# Bedtime Stories for Fearless Girls

## Tales of Trailblazers Like You Who Changed the World

## By Ali O'Connor

## Disclaimer Notice:

# Table of Contents

# Are you ready to dream?

As you get ready to go to sleep, let's read this story together. Each chapter is a tale of a real woman who made her mark on the world. From ancient queens to modern-day activists, these women have overcome obstacles, been the first in their field, and inspired change.

We will learn about different female icons, from their childhood and early career to their biggest achievements and contributions. These stories will inspire and motivate you to follow your heart. You can be an actress, gymnast, scientist, or anything else you can dream of as long as you believe in yourself.

Sleep well, and chase your dreams!

# Naomi Osaka

Once upon a time, there was a young girl just like you who lived in Chuo-ku, Osaka, Japan. Her name was Naomi Osaka. Naomi loved to play a game called tennis. She would play it every day and even compete in big tournaments all around the world.

As she grew up, Naomi became really good at tennis and even won many big trophies. She was known for her strong shots and her never give up attitude.

Naomi was also known for using her special game to help others, she would wear special masks with the names of people who were not treated fairly.

But Naomi faced some tough times too, she had to take a break from tennis because she was feeling sad and anxious. But she didn't give up, she took care of herself and came back stronger.

Naomi continues to play tennis and inspires many people with her hard work and kindness.

Did you like Naomi's story, what do you think makes her special?

Now, close your eyes and drift off to sleep, let your dreams take you on a magical adventure. Sleep tight.

# Michelle Obama

Once upon a time, there was a young girl just like you who lived in Chicago, Illinois, USA. Her name was Michelle Obama. Michelle loved to read and learn new things. She was very smart and worked hard in school.

As she grew up, Michelle became a lawyer and helped people who were not treated fairly. She also met a man named Barack Obama who became the President of the United States. She was the First Lady and she used her special job to help children like you.

Michelle also wrote a book about her life and how she became who she is. She also started a program called "Let's Move" to help kids eat healthy and be active.

She also traveled around the world to talk to people and spread kindness and love. She is a great role model for many people.

What was your favorite part of Michelle Obama's story?

Now, close your eyes, drift off to sleep and let your dreams take you on a wonderful adventure. Sleep tight.

# Rhianna

Once upon a time, there was a young girl just like you who lived in a place called Barbados. Her name was Rhianna. Rhianna loved to sing and make music. She would sing all the time, and even write her own songs.

As she grew older, Rhianna became really good at singing and making music. She would sing in big concert halls and on television shows, and people all over the world would listen to her music.

Rhianna was also known for her sense of style, she would wear really cool clothes and make-up, and people would look up to her for fashion inspiration.

But Rhianna faced some tough times too, she went through difficult situations but she never gave up. She continued to make music and inspire people with her voice and her words.

Rhianna has several businesses to design clothes and she's also involved in charity work.

What did you like about Rhianna's story, what was most interesting? Now, close your eyes and drift off to sleep, let your dreams take you on a magical adventure. Sleep tight.

# Greta Thunberg

Once upon a time, there was a young girl just like you who lived in a place called Sweden. Her name was Greta. Greta was very concerned about the world and the environment. She believed that everyone should take care of the planet and make sure it's healthy for everyone and everything living in it.

Greta started to speak up about her concerns and even did something called a "strike" where she would miss school to protest and call attention to the issue. Her actions inspired many other young people to do the same and speak up for the planet.

Greta traveled all around the world, talking to grown-ups, and leaders, and even went on a boat trip across the ocean to talk about how to make the earth better.

Greta never gave up on her message and continues to spread awareness and inspire people of all ages to take action and make a change.

Does Greta's story inspire you, what did you find interesting in her story?

Now, close your eyes, drift off to sleep and let your dreams take you on a wonderful adventure. Sleep tight.

# Sarah Al-Amiri

Once upon a time, there was a young girl just like you who lived in the city of Dubai in the United Arab Emirates. Her name was Sarah Al-Amiri. Sarah loved learning about science and space. She would read books and watch videos about it all the time.

As she grew older, Sarah became really smart and knew a lot about space. She even helped lead a team that sent a spacecraft to Mars! The spacecraft sent back important information and pictures of Mars that scientists all over the world used to learn more about the planet.

Sarah was also an important leader in her country, she held a position as the Minister of Advanced Sciences and helped make important decisions for her country.

Sarah was determined to make sure that everyone, including young girls like you, had the chance to learn about and be inspired by science and space.

What do you think makes Sarah Al-Amiri interesting? Now, close your eyes, drift off to sleep and let your dreams take you on a wonderful adventure. Sleep tight.

# Malala Yousafzai

Once upon a time, there was a young girl just like you who lived in a small village called Mingora in Pakistan. Her name was Malala.

Malala loved learning and going to school, but one day, some mean people didn't want girls to go to school anymore. Malala spoke out and said that girls have the right to learn just like boys do.

Because of this, the mean people hurt Malala by shooting her in the head. But Malala was very brave and strong, and she got better. She didn't give up on her dream of education for all girls.

Malala went on to become a famous education advocate, traveling the world and speaking to many important people. She even won a special prize called the Nobel Peace Prize for her work.

Did you think Malala was brave, what did you find most interesting about her story?

Now, close your eyes, drift off to sleep and let your dreams take you on a wonderful adventure. Sleep tight.

# Simone Biles

Once upon a time, there was a young girl just like you who lived in Spring, Texas, USA. Her name was Simone Biles. Simone loved gymnastics and would practice every day. She was very good at it and competed in big gymnastics competitions all over the world.

As she grew up, Simone became one of the best gymnasts in the world. She won many big medals, including five Olympic medals and 19 World Championship medals. She was known for her powerful tumbling and her hardworking attitude.

Simone was also known for her courage and determination. She had to overcome many obstacles and challenges on her way to the top, but she never gave up. She was a role model for many young gymnasts, who looked up to her and were inspired by her.

Despite her success, Simone always remained humble and grateful, she always acknowledged her teammates, coaches and support system.

What do you think makes Simone Biles special? Now, close your eyes and drift off to sleep, let your dreams take you on a magical adventure. Sleep tight.

# Alexandria Ocasio-Cortez

Once upon a time there was a young girl just like you who lived in the Bronx, New York City. Her name was Alexandria. Alexandria grew up in a big city and she saw that many people were not treated fairly. She wanted to do something to help make things better for everyone.

As she grew up, Alexandria became a leader who helps people in her community. She would stand up for what is right and make sure that everyone had a chance to have their voices heard. She worked hard to make sure that everyone had access to things like good schools, healthcare, and clean water.

Alexandria also became a congresswoman, which means she helps make the laws for the whole country. She continues to work hard to make sure that everyone is treated fairly and has the same opportunities.

What do you think was interesting about Alexandria's story?

Now, close your eyes, drift off to sleep, and let your dreams take you on a beautiful adventure. Sleep tight.

# Maria Tallchief

Once upon a time, there was a young girl just like you who lived in Fairfax, Oklahoma, United States. Her name was Maria Tallchief. Maria loved to dance and would practice every day. She grew up to be one of the most famous ballet dancers in the world.

Maria danced in many big shows and even in the famous New York City Ballet. She was the first Native American prima ballerina, which means she was the best dancer in the company.

Maria was known for her grace and beauty on stage, she would make the audience feel like they were watching a magical story unfold before their eyes.

Despite facing some challenges as a Native American woman who was dancing with mostly white people, Maria never gave up on her dream to dance and she became an inspiration for many young dancers.

What did you love about the story of Maria Tallchief?

Now, close your eyes and drift off to sleep, let your dreams take you on a wonderful dance adventure. Sleep tight.

# Shonda Rhimes

Once upon a time there was a young girl just like you who lived in Park Forest, Illinois, USA. Her name was Shonda Rhimes. Shonda loved writing stories and making shows. She would write stories and make shows that were fun and had important messages.

As she grew up, Shonda became a very famous writer and show maker. She made many popular shows like "Grey's Anatomy" She was known for creating strong and interesting characters, especially women and people of color, and for writing stories that tackle important issues like race and gender.

Shonda also used her platform to inspire and empower other young girls and women who wanted to pursue careers in the entertainment industry.

But Shonda faced some challenges, she had to work very hard to break into the industry and be successful. But she never gave up, she kept writing and making shows that she believed in.

What do you think makes Shonda Rhimes interesting?

Now, close your eyes, drift off to sleep, and let your dreams take you on a magical adventure. Sleep tight.

# Karren Brady

Once upon a time there was a young girl just like you who lived in London, England. Her name was Karren Brady. Karren loved sports and she was very good at it. She always wanted to be in charge of a sports team.

As she got older, Karren became one of the most important people in a big football team called West Ham United. She was in charge of making sure the team had everything they needed and was also in charge of making important decisions for the team.

Karren was also known for being very successful in her job, she was the first woman to hold such a high position in a football club.

She was also a role model for many young girls showing them that they can accomplish anything they set their minds to, regardless of their gender.

Despite facing some challenges, Karren never gave up on her dream of being in charge of a sports team. She worked hard and became one of the most successful women in sports.

What did you think of Karren Brady's story?

Now, close your eyes, drift off to sleep and let your dreams take you on a fantastic adventure. Sleep tight.

# Phoebe Schecter

Once upon a time, a young girl like you loved nothing more than playing sports. She was fast, agile, and had a competitive spirit that couldn't be beat. Her name was Phoebe Schecter and she dreamed of one day becoming a coach for her favorite sport.

As she grew older, Phoebe worked hard to develop her skills and knowledge of the game. She studied strategies and techniques, and practiced tirelessly to improve her own performance. And her hard work paid off.

One day, Phoebe received an exciting opportunity to join the Buffalo Bills as their Coaching Intern. She was thrilled to have the chance to work with such a talented team and learn from some of the best coaches in the business.

Phoebe quickly proved herself to be an asset to the team. She was dedicated, hardworking, and always willing to go the extra mile to help her players succeed. It wasn't long before she was promoted to Tight Ends Coach, making her the first female coach in the history of the Buffalo Bills.

Now, close your eyes and dream of all the amazing things you will achieve one day. Goodnight.

# Jane Goodall

Once upon a time, there was a young girl just like you who lived in London, England. Her name was Jane Goodall. Jane loved animals so much that she wanted to learn everything about them. She studied about them, read books about them and even wanted to live with them.

When Jane grew up, she went to Africa and met a special group of animals called chimpanzees. She spent many years living with the chimpanzees and learning all about them. She learned that they had emotions, they used tools, and they even had their own communities and families.

Jane also worked very hard to protect the chimpanzees and their homes. She helped to create a special place called Gombe Stream National Park where the chimpanzees could live safely.

Jane spent many years in Africa and eventually moved back to England, but she continued to work hard to protect animals and their homes. She traveled the world to talk about the importance of protecting animals and the environment.

What do you think Jane Goodall was most surprised to learn about the chimpanzees?

Now, close your eyes and drift off to sleep, let your dreams take you on a magical adventure. Sleep tight.

# Ann Daniels

Once upon a time, there was a young girl just like you named Ann who lived in a small village in the United Kingdom. Ann loved adventure and exploring new places. She loved to go on hikes in the mountains and go camping in the woods.

Ann grew up to be an explorer and went on many exciting trips to faraway places. She traveled to the North and South poles, and even went on a journey to the top of the highest mountain in the world, Mount Everest. She faced many challenges, like the cold weather and the high altitude, but she never gave up.

Ann also loved to share her adventures with others, she would take pictures and write about her trips so that people could learn about the different places she visited and the animals she saw.

Ann was a brave and determined adventurer, she inspired many people to follow their dreams and never give up.

What do you think Ann's favorite part of her adventure was?

Now, close your eyes, drift off to sleep and let your dreams take you on a wonderful adventure. Sleep tight.

# Emma Watson

Once upon a time, a young girl like you lived in England. Her name was Emma Watson and she loved reading books, especially stories about brave and independent young girls.

As she grew older, Emma became interested in acting and started taking acting classes. She worked hard to improve her craft and eventually landed a role in a famous movie series about a boy wizard.

Emma's portrayal of Hermione, the clever and courageous young witch, became very popular with people all over the world. She loved being able to entertain and inspire others through her acting.

But Emma also wanted to use her platform to make a difference in the world. She became a vocal advocate for gender equality and women's rights, giving powerful speeches and using her voice to raise awareness on important issues.

Through her acting and activism, Emma became a role model for young girls everywhere. She showed that it is possible to be passionate about your career and also use your talents to make a positive impact on the world.

So, if you have a dream or a cause that you care about, don't be afraid to speak up and make your voice heard. You never know what kind of difference you might be able to make. Just like Emma, you have the power to inspire others and make a positive impact on the world.

Now, close your eyes and drift off to sleep, dreaming of all the amazing things you will achieve one day. Goodnight.

# AbiSoye Ajayi-Akinfolarin

Once upon a time, there was a young girl just like you who lived in Lagos, Nigeria. Her name was Abisoye. Abisoye loved to learn about computers and how they work. She would spend hours reading books and watching videos about coding.

As she grew older, Abisoye became really good at coding. She even started teaching other girls in her community how to code too! She believed that girls should have the same opportunities as boys to learn about technology and have a chance to have jobs in the tech industry.

Abisoye started a program called "GirlsCoding" to teach girls in her community how to code and learn about computers. She also worked to change the perception that girls should not be involved in the tech industry.

Abisoye's work inspired many young girls in her community to learn about technology and pursue their dreams.

What do you think makes Abisoye special?

Now, close your eyes and drift off to sleep, let your dreams take you on a magical adventure. Sleep tight.

# Jennifer Lawrence

Once upon a time there was a young girl just like you who lived in Louisville, Kentucky, USA. Her name was Jennifer Lawrence. Jennifer loved acting and she was very good at it. She would practice and perform in plays and shows.

As she got older, Jennifer became one of the most famous actresses in the world. She acted in movies like "The Hunger Games" and "Silver Linings Playbook" and won many big awards. She was known for her talent and her fun personality.

Jennifer also helped other people through her work, she supported many charities and causes.

Despite her success, Jennifer faced some challenges in her career too. She had to work very hard to become an actress and she had to learn to handle fame.

Despite her challenges, Jennifer never gave up on her dream of being an actress. She worked hard and remained humble and kind. She continues to inspire people all over the world with her talent and her generosity.

What do you think makes Jennifer Lawrence special?

Now, close your eyes, drift off to sleep and let your dreams take you on a wonderful adventure. Sleep tight.

# Venus and Serena Williams

Once upon a time, there were two young girls named Venus and Serena who lived in a place called California in the United States. They loved to play a game called tennis. They would play it every day and even compete in big tournaments all around the world.

As they grew up, Venus and Serena became really good at tennis and even won many big trophies. They were known for their strong shots and their never give up attitude. They would often play against each other in big tournaments, but they were still best friends.

Venus and Serena were also known for using their special game to help others. They worked hard to make sure that everyone had the opportunity to play tennis, no matter who they were.

But Venus and Serena faced some tough times too, they had to take breaks from tennis because they were feeling tired or injured. But they didn't give up, they took care of themselves and came back stronger.

Venus and Serena continue to play tennis and inspire many people with their hard work and kindness.

What do you think makes these sisters special?

Now, close your eyes and drift off to sleep, let your dreams take you on a magical adventure. Sleep tight.

# Ada Lovelace

Once upon a time, there was a young girl just like you who lived in London, England. Her name was Ada Lovelace. Ada was very smart and loved to learn about numbers and how things worked.

When she grew up, Ada became friends with a man named Charles Babbage. Charles had an idea for a special machine that could do math problems very quickly. Ada helped Charles understand how the machine could do even more than just math, it could also be used to create pictures and music.

Ada wrote about Charles' machine and her ideas in a book. Her writing was so special and important that people still read it today. Ada is considered the first computer programmer because of her work on Charles' machine.

Ada's ideas and writing have helped many people understand how machines can be used in different ways.

What do you think makes Ada special?

Now, close your eyes and drift off to sleep, let your dreams take you on a magical adventure. Sleep tight.

# Margaret Hamilton

Once upon a time, there was a young girl just like you who lived in Indiana, United States. Her name was Margaret Hamilton. Margaret loved math and science when she was growing up. She would always ask questions and try to figure out how things worked.

As she got older, Margaret became a computer scientist. She worked at a big company called NASA, and helped put the Apollo spaceship on the moon. She made sure all the instructions for the spaceship were correct and in order, kind of like a cook following a recipe.

But Margaret also faced a big challenge, the computer on the spaceship was very small and not enough memory, she worked hard and found a way to make the instructions fit, and the spaceship was able to land on the moon safely.

Margaret was a pioneer in her field and helped pave the way for many other women to pursue careers in technology.

What do you think Margaret Hamilton was most excited about?

Now, close your eyes and drift off to sleep, let your dreams take you on a brilliant adventure. Sleep tight.

# Cleopatra

Once upon a time, a young girl like you lived in ancient Egypt. Her name was Cleopatra and she was the daughter of the Pharaoh. From a young age, Cleopatra was intelligent and ambitious. She studied hard, learning about history, science, and politics.

As she grew older, Cleopatra became more and more interested in ruling her kingdom. She knew that she had the skills and determination to lead her people, and she was determined to prove it. And eventually, she became the first woman to rule Egypt on her own.

Cleopatra was a powerful and wise queen, making fair and just decisions for her people. She also worked to improve her kingdom's economy and culture, building new temples and libraries and encouraging trade with other countries.

But Cleopatra's rule was not always easy. She faced many challenges and had to fight hard to protect her kingdom. But she never let those challenges stop her. She remained determined and strong and always stood up for what she believed in.  Cleopatra became one of the most famous queens in history

Now, close your eyes and drift off to sleep, let your dreams take you on a brilliant adventure. Sleep tight.

# J.K. Rowling

Once upon a time, there was a young girl just like you who lived in a place called England. Her name was J.K. Rowling. J.K. loved to read and write stories. She would always have a book with her and would spend hours writing her own stories.

As she grew older, J.K. wanted to share her stories with others, but many people said "no" to publishing her book. They didn't think it was good enough. But J.K. didn't give up. She kept writing and sending her book to different publishers.

Finally, one publisher said "yes" and decided to give J.K.'s book a chance. And that's how the Harry Potter series was born. The story of a young wizard and his friends at a magical school captivated readers around the world and became a beloved classic.

J.K. Rowling's hard work paid off and her books became very popular, people all over the world loved them!

What do you think makes J.K. Rowling's stories special?

Now, close your eyes, drift off to sleep and let your dreams take you on a wonderful adventure. Sleep tight.

# Barbara Walters

Once upon a time, there was a young girl just like you who lived in Boston, Massachusetts, USA. Her name was Barbara Walters. Barbara loved to talk to people and learn about their stories.

As she grew up, Barbara became a very famous television host. She talked to many important people like presidents and movie stars. She asked them questions and helped people learn more about them.

Barbara was also the first woman to co-anchor a national evening news program and the first woman to anchor a evening news program by herself. She was a trailblazer in the industry, breaking many barriers for women in television.

But Barbara faced some challenges in her career too, she had to work very hard to be taken seriously as a news anchor because people didn't think women could do that job. But she never gave up and proved everyone wrong.

What do you think makes Barbara Walters interesting?

Now, close your eyes and drift off to sleep, let your dreams take you on a magical adventure. Sleep tight.

# Katharine Graham

Once upon a time, there was a young girl just like you who lived in New York City, United States. Her name was Katharine Graham. Katharine was very curious and loved to read newspapers and books.

As she grew up, Katharine became the boss of a big newspaper called The Washington Post. She made sure that the newspaper told the truth and helped people learn about important things happening in the world.

Katharine was also very brave, she stood up for what was right even when people were trying to make her be quiet. She helped to reveal a secret government plan called Watergate, which helped many people know the truth.

Katharine was a trailblazer for women, she was one of the first women to be in charge of a big newspaper and she set a great example for other women to follow.

What do you think makes Katharine Graham interesting?

Now, close your eyes and drift off to sleep, let your dreams take you on a magical adventure. Sleep tight.

# Sally Ride

Once upon a time there was a young girl just like you who lived in Encino, California, USA. Her name was Sally Ride. Sally loved science and learning about space. She studied hard and worked hard to become an astronaut.

Sally grew up to be the first American woman to go to space. She flew on a spaceship called the Space Shuttle Challenger in 1983. She helped scientists learn more about space and how it works.

Sally also helped other girls and women to dream big and to know they can do anything they set their minds to.

Sally was a very special person, She was an astronaut, a teacher and an author. She inspired many people to learn more about space and to never give up on their dreams.

What do you think makes Sally Ride special?

Now, close your eyes, drift off to sleep and let your dreams take you on a wonderful adventure. Sleep tight.

# Grace Hopper

Once upon a time, there was a young girl just like you who lived in New York, United States. Her name was Grace Hopper. Grace was very interested in math and numbers, and she loved to play with machines that could do many things, like adding and subtracting.

When Grace grew up, she became a very important person in the Navy. She worked with special machines that helped the Navy do important work, like talking to other ships and planes. She also helped to create a special computer language called COBOL that many people still use today to talk to computers.

Grace was a hard worker and always wanted to learn more. She was also a Rear Admiral in the Navy, which is a very high rank. She was the first woman to hold that rank.

Grace never gave up on her dream of working with computers and helping the Navy. She inspired many people with her hard work and determination.

What do you think makes Grace Hopper special?

Now, close your eyes, drift off to sleep and let your dreams take you on a wonderful adventure. Sleep tight.

# Harriet Tubman

Once upon a time, there was a young girl just like you who lived in Maryland, United States. Her name was Harriet Tubman. Harriet was born into slavery, which means she was owned by someone else and had to work for them without getting paid.

Harriet knew that this was not fair and she wanted to be free. So, when she was older, she escaped from slavery and went on a journey to freedom. Along the way, she helped many other slaves escape too, using a secret network of safe houses and trails called the Underground Railroad.

Harriet was very brave and resourceful, she led hundreds of enslaved people to freedom, and even served as a scout and spy for the Union army during the Civil War.

Harriet Tubman's courage and determination helped change the course of history and made our world a better place.

What do you think makes Harriet Tubman a special person?

Now, close your eyes and drift off to sleep, let your dreams take you on a magical adventure. Sleep tight.

# Clara Barton

Once upon a time, there was a young girl just like you who lived in North Oxford, Massachusetts, USA. Her name was Clara Barton. Clara was a very kind and caring person, who loved to help others.

When she grew up, Clara became a nurse and helped many people who were hurt or sick. She even went to war zones to take care of soldiers during the Civil War. Clara worked hard to make sure they had the medicine and supplies they needed to get better.

After the war, Clara helped create an organization called the American Red Cross. It's a group of people who help others during emergencies and disasters. Clara also helped set up schools and libraries in places where children didn't have access to education.

Clara was a very determined person and never gave up in her efforts to help others. She traveled around the world, helping those in need, and was known as the "Angel of the Battlefield."

What do you think Clara Barton did to help others?

Now, close your eyes and drift off to sleep, let your dreams take you on a wonderful adventure. Sleep tight.

# Indira Gandhi

Once upon a time, there was a young girl named Indira who lived in India. She grew up to be a leader, just like the grown-ups in her village.

Indira worked hard and helped many people in her country. She made sure that everyone had enough food to eat, and that children could go to school. She also worked to make India a stronger country by building factories and roads.

Indira was a strong leader, but sometimes her decision were not always popular. Nevertheless, she kept working hard for her country and its people.

Indira was also the first woman to lead India, she broke down barriers for women and showed that they can be leaders too.

What do you think Indira Gandhi did that made her special?

Now, close your eyes and drift off to sleep, let your dreams take you on a magical adventure. Sleep tight

# Valentina Tereshkova

Once upon a time, there was a young girl just like you who lived in a small village in Russia. Her name was Valentina Tereshkova. Valentina loved to look up at the sky and watch the stars. She dreamed of one day flying high up in the air like a bird.

Valentina grew up and became a pilot. She flew airplanes and even went to space! She was the first woman in the world to ever go to space. She flew on a special spaceship called Vostok 6 and spent three whole days in space!

Valentina had a very important mission while she was in space, she flew around the Earth 48 times, took photographs and collected important information about space.

Valentina's journey in space was not easy, she faced many challenges and dangers, but she was brave and determined to complete her mission.

Valentina's journey to space was a big milestone in history, she inspired many young girls to follow their dreams and chase their aspirations.

What do you think was the most interesting thing about Valentina Tereshkova's story?

Now, close your eyes, drift off to sleep and let your dreams take you on a wonderful adventure. Sleep tight.

# Ruth Bader Ginsburg

Once upon a time there was a young girl just like you who lived in Brooklyn, New York, USA. Her name was Ruth Bader Ginsburg. Ruth loved to learn and read books. She studied hard and went to many schools.

As she grew older, Ruth became a very important lady. She was a judge and helped make sure everyone was treated fairly. She worked very hard to make sure that girls and boys, men and women, all had the same rights and opportunities. She even became a judge on the highest court in the land called the Supreme Court.

Ruth was also known for her kindness and her love for her family. Even when she was very busy, she always made time for her loved ones.

Ruth passed away in 2020, but her legacy and the change she brought will always be remembered.

What do you think made Ruth Bader Ginsburg special?

Now, close your eyes, drift off to sleep and let your dreams take you on a wonderful adventure. Sleep tight.

# Dorothy Levitt

Once upon a time there was a young girl just like you who lived in London, England. Her name was Dorothy Levitt. Dorothy loved cars and she was very good at driving them. She would go for rides every day and compete in car races all over the world.

As she got older, Dorothy became one of the first women to compete in car races and also she became a car demonstrator. She broke many records and was known for her speed and her daring on the race track.

Dorothy was also known for using her platform to promote women's rights to drive. She wrote a book called "The Woman and the Car" which encouraged women to learn to drive and to be independent.

Dorothy was a trailblazer in her time, she was a true inspiration for many women.

What do you think makes Dorothy interesting?

Now, close your eyes, drift off to sleep and let your dreams take you on a wonderful adventure. Sleep tight.

# Rosalind Franklin

Once upon a time, there was a young girl just like you who lived in London, England. Her name was Rosalind Franklin. Rosalind loved science and exploring the world around her. She wanted to learn as much as she could about the tiny things that make up everything we see.

Rosalind went to school and studied hard to become a scientist. She learned about crystals and how they are made. She took pictures of crystals using a special machine called X-ray diffraction.

She took a photograph called Photo 51 which was very important for the discovery of the structure of DNA. Her work helped others to understand how the building blocks of life are put together.

Even though Rosalind passed away before the discovery of DNA structure was awarded the Nobel Prize, her contributions were acknowledged as vital part of the discovery.

What do you think about Rosalind Franklin's contribution to the discovery of DNA?

Now, close your eyes, drift off to sleep and let your dreams take you on a wonderful adventure. Sleep tight.

# Chien-Shiung Wu

Once upon a time, there was a young girl just like you who lived in Liuhe, Taicang, China. Her name was Chien-Shiung Wu. Chien-Shiung loved to learn and discover new things, especially about science.

As she grew older, Chien-Shiung became a very smart scientist and studied a subject called physics. She helped discover something important called "beta decay" and was known as the "First Lady of Physics"

But it was not easy for Chien-Shiung, in her time it was harder for girls and women to become scientists. But she didn't let that stop her, she worked hard and showed the world that girls can be scientists too!

Chien-Shiung also used her knowledge to make special tools called "Geiger counters" that were used to measure radiation and they are used today in factories and hospitals.

Chien-Shiung's discoveries and hard work continue to inspire many scientists today.

What do you think Chien-Shiung Wu is known for?

Now, close your eyes and drift off to sleep, let your dreams take you on a fantastic adventure. Sleep tight.

Made in the USA
Las Vegas, NV
28 December 2024